# THE VICTORIAN AGE

# THE
# VICTORIAN AGE

*The Rede Lecture for* 1922

BY

WILLIAM RALPH INGE,
C.V.O., D.D., D.Litt., F.B.A.

HON. FELLOW OF JESUS COLLEGE

CAMBRIDGE
AT THE UNIVERSITY PRESS
1922

# CAMBRIDGE
## UNIVERSITY PRESS

University Printing House, Cambridge CB2 8BS, United Kingdom

Cambridge University Press is part of the University of Cambridge.

It furthers the University's mission by disseminating knowledge in the pursuit of
education, learning and research at the highest international levels of excellence.

www.cambridge.org
Information on this title: www.cambridge.org/9781107495098

© Cambridge University Press 1922

First published 1922
First paperback edition 2015

A catalogue record for this publication is available from the British Library

ISBN 978-1-107-49509-8 Paperback

# THE VICTORIAN AGE

EACH generation takes a special pleasure in removing the household gods of its parents from their pedestals, and consigning them to the cupboard. The prophet or pioneer, after being at first declared to be unintelligible or absurd, has a brief spell of popularity, after which he is said to be conventional, and then antiquated. We may find more than one reason for this. A movement has more to fear from its disciples than from its critics. The great man is linked to his age by his weakest side; and his epigoni, who are not great men, caricature his message and make it ridiculous. Besides, every movement is a reaction, and generates counter-reactions. The pendulum swings backwards and forwards. Every institution not only carries within it the seeds of its own dissolution, but prepares the way for its most hated rival.

The German Von Eicken found, in this tendency of all human movements to provoke violent reactions, the master key of history. Every idea or institution passes into its opposite. For instance, Roman imperialism, which was created by an intense national consciousness, ended by destroying the nationality of rulers and subjects alike. The fanatical nationalism of the Jews left them a people without a country. The Catholic Church began by renouncing the world, and became the heir of the defunct Roman empire. In political philosophy, the law of the swinging pendulum may act as a salutary cold douche. Universal suffrage, says Sybel, has always heralded the end of parliamentary government. Tocqueville caps this by saying that the more successful a democracy is in levelling a population, the less will be the resistance which the next despotism will encounter.

But the pendulum sometimes swings very slowly, and oscillates within narrow limits; while at other times the changes are violent and rapid. The last century and a half, beginning with what Arnold

Toynbee was the first to call the Industrial Revolution, has been a period of more rapid change than any other which history records. The French Revolution, which coincided with its first stages, helped to break the continuity between the old order and the new, and both by its direct influence and by the vigorous reactions which it generated cleft society into conflicting elements. Then followed a Great War, which shook the social structure to its base, and awakened into intense vitality the slumbering enthusiasm of nationality. At the same time, a variety of mechanical inventions gave man an entirely new control over the forces of nature and a new knowledge of the laws of nature, and this new knowledge, not content with practical applications, soon revolutionised all the natural sciences, and profoundly affected both religion and philosophy. The reign of Queen Victoria, which I have chosen to mark the limits of my survey to-day, covered the latter half of this *saeculum mirabile*, the most wonderful century in human history.

There are of course no beginnings or ends in history. We may walk for a few miles by the side of a river, noting its shallows and its rapids, the gorges which confine it and the plains through which it meanders; but we know that we have seen neither the beginning nor the end of its course, that the whole river has an unbroken continuity, and that sections, whether of space or time, are purely arbitrary. We are always sowing our future; we are always reaping our past. The Industrial Revolution began in reality before the accession of George III, and the French monarchy was stricken with mortal disease before Louis XV bequeathed his kingdom to his luckless successor.

But there can be no question that the river of civilisation reached a stretch of rapids towards the end of the eighteenth century. For instance, in locomotion the riding-horse and pack-horse had hardly given place to the coach and waggon before the railway superseded road traffic; the fast sailing clippers had a short lease of life before steam was used for crossing the seas. Industrial changes came too quickly for the government to make the necessary readjustments, at a time when the nation was fighting for its life and then recovering from its exhaustion. The greatest sufferings caused by the revolution in the life of the people were in the first half of the century ; the latter half was a time of readjustment and reform. One great interest of the Victorian Age is that it was the time when a new social order was being built up, and entirely new problems were being solved. The nineteenth century has been called the age of hope ; and perhaps only a superstitious belief in the automatic progress of humanity could have carried our fathers and grandfathers through the tremendous difficulties which the rush through the rapids imposed upon them.

Let us spend five minutes in picturing to ourselves the English nation in a condition of stable equilibrium, as it was in the eighteenth century. Before the Industrial Revolution, the country was on the whole prosperous and contented.

The masses had no voice in the government, but most of them had a stake in the country. There were no large towns, and the typical unit was the self-contained village, which included craftsmen as well as agriculturists, and especially workers in wool, the staple national industry. The aim of village agriculture was to provide subsistence for the parishioners, not to feed the towns. The typical village was a street of cottages, each with a small garden, and an open field round it, divided up like a modern allotments area. The roads between villages were mere tracks across the common, often so bad that carts were driven by preference through the fields, as they still are in Greece. So each parish provided for its own needs. The population was sparse, and increased very slowly, in spite of the enormous birthrate, because the majority of the children died. Families like that of Dean Colet, who was one of twenty-two children, among whom he was the only one to grow up, remained common till the middle of the eighteenth century. Then, for reasons which have never, I think, been fully explained, the deathrate rapidly declined, at the very time when economic conditions demanded a larger population. This is the more remarkable, when we remember the manner in which young children were treated before the Factory Acts.

Political power was in the hands of a genuine aristocracy, who did more to deserve their privileges than any other aristocracy of modern times. They were, as a class, highly cultivated men, who had travelled much on the Continent, and mixed in society there. In 1785 Gibbon was told that 40,000 English were either travelling or living abroad at one time. They were enlightened patrons of literature and art, and made the collections of masterpieces which were the pride of England, and which are now being dispersed to the winds. Their libraries were well stocked, and many of them were accomplished classical scholars. They were not content, like their successors to-day, to load their tables with magazines and newspapers.

Lastly, they fought Napoleon to a finish, and never showed the white feather. Those who have studied the family portraits in a great house, or the wonderful portrait gallery in the Provost's Lodge at Eton, will see on the faces not only the pride and self-satisfaction of a privileged class, but the power to lead the nation whether in the arts of war or of peace.

No doubt, political corruption was rampant; but it was not till George III tried to govern himself by means of corruption, that its consequences were disastrous. The loss of America was the first serious blow to the aristocratic régime.

The necessary changes would have come about earlier but for the French Revolution and the war. The former caused a panic which now seems to us exaggerated. But we are accustomed to revolutions, and know that they never last more than a few years; the French Revolution was the first of its kind. Moreover, France had long been the acknowledged leader of civilisation, and

a general overturn in that country ter-
rified men like Gibbon into prophesying
that a similar outbreak was likely to
overwhelm law, order and property in
England. They did not realise how
different the conditions were in the two
countries. The most modest democratic
reforms were therefore impossible till
Napoleon was out of the way, and till the
anti-revolutionary panic had subsided.

One result of the war has not always
been realised. The eighteenth century
had been international; there was no
Chauvinism or Jingoism anywhere till
the French, fighting ostensibly under the
banner of humanity, had kindled the fire
of patriotism in Spain, in Germany, and
even in Russia. England had always had
a strong national self-consciousness; and
after the war the bonds of sympathy with
France were not at once renewed, so that
our country, during the early part of
Victoria's reign, was more isolated from
the main currents of European thought
than ever before or since. Men of letters
who lamented this isolation now turned
for inspiration rather to Germany than

to France. On the other hand, the war
did not interrupt the intellectual life of
the country to anything like the same
extent as the recent Great War. At no
period since the Elizabethans was there
such an output of great poetry; and it
does not seem to have occurred to any
young lady of that time to ask Scott,
Wordsworth or Jane Austen what they
were doing during the war.

Modern sociologists have drawn lurid
pictures of the condition of the working
class during the earlier part of the last
century. It seems in truth to have been
very bad. Byron in 1812 told the Lords:
'I have been in some of the most op-
pressed provinces of Turkey, but never
under the most despotic of infidel governments did I behold such squalid wretched-
ness as I have seen since my return in the
very heart of a Christian country.' In
1831 a member of parliament said: 'An
agricultural labourer and a pauper—the
words are synonymous.' Those who want
details can find them in the well-known
controversial books by the Hammonds,
which state the case against the govern-

ing class in an exhaustive manner. There was in fact too much ground for Disraeli's statement that England at that time consisted of two nations, the rich and the poor. The poor were still largely illiterate, and so inarticulate; and the comparative absence of the large half-educated class which now dominates all public discussion made the cultivated gentry a class apart. Their own standard of culture was higher than that of the leisured class to-day; but they took little interest in the lives of the poor, until they were forced to do so. We however who have witnessed the succession of economic crises which attend and follow a great war ought not to forget the appalling difficulties with which the government was confronted. In 1795 there was actual famine, which was met by the famous system of doles out of the rates, in augmentation of wages, a most mischievous bit of legislation, like the similar expedients of the last three years. It had the double effect of pauperising the rural labourer and of putting an artificial premium on large families—the children who were carted off in waggon-loads to feed the factories. It was repealed only when the ruined farmers were abandoning their land, and the glebe-owning clergy their livings. Fluctuations in prices had much to do with the miseries of the hungry thirties and forties; but over-population, as the economists of the time pointed out with perfect justice, was one of the main causes. It was not till much later that there was food enough for all; and this was the result of the new wheat fields of America and the sheep walks of Australia, which brought in food and took away mouths. In Ireland the barbarous and illiterate peasantry multiplied till the population exceeded eight millions, when the inevitable famine illustrated nature's method of dealing with recklessness. The only error with which the economists of this time may be charged was that they did not realise that over-population is the result of a very low standard of civilisation. Families are restricted whenever the parents have social ambitions and a standard of comfort. Where they have none, the vital statistics are those of Russia, Ireland, India and China.

The astonishing progress in all measurable values which marked the first half of the reign produced a whole literature of complacency. I quoted some examples of the language which was then common, in my Romanes Lecture on 'The Idea of Progress.' Macaulay supplies some of the best examples. We must remember that the progress was real, and that its speed was unexampled in history. The country was, in vulgar language, a going concern, as it never was before and has not been since. The dominions beyond the seas were being peopled up and consolidated. At home education was spreading, liberty was increasing, and the light taxes were raised with an ease which fortunately for ourselves we no longer even remember. Principles seemed to have been discovered which guaranteed a further advance in almost every direction, intellectual as well as material. For that was the great age of British science; and most branches of literature were flourishing. Hope told a flattering tale, and optimism became a sort of religion.

Nevertheless, such complacency was

bound to produce a violent protest. Disraeli, whose well-remembered warning about 'the two nations' has already been quoted, described the age as one which by the help of mechanical inventions had mistaken comfort for progress. And comfort, as another critic of social science has said, is more insidious than luxury in hampering the higher development of a people. The literature of social indignation was contemporaneous with the literature of complacency. Carlyle and Ruskin were its chief prophets; but we must not forget the novels of Dickens, Charles Reade and Kingsley.

Carlyle and Ruskin both denounced the age with the vehemence of major prophets—vehemence was in fashion at that time in English literature—but they did not approach the 'condition of England question' from quite the same angle. Carlyle was a Stoic, or in other words a Calvinist without dogmas; he had also learned to be a mystic from his studies of German idealism. He represents one phase of the anti-French reaction; he hated most of the ideas of 1789, as displayed in their results. He hated the scepticism of the Revolution, its negations, its love of claptrap rhetoric and fine phrases, and above all its anarchism. He wished to see society well ordered, under its wisest men; he wished to overcome materialism by idealism, and loose morality by industry and the fear of God. Justice, he declared, is done in this world; right is might, if we take long views. Institutions collapse when they become shams, and no longer fulfil their function. The sporting squires ought to be founding colonies instead of preserving game. As for the new industrialism, he disliked it with the fervour of a Scottish peasant.

Ruskin was a Platonist, steeped in the study of Plato, and bound to him by complete sympathy. We cannot separate Ruskin the art-critic from Ruskin the social reformer. His great discovery was the close connection of the decay of art with faulty social arrangements. Ugliness in the works of man is a symptom of social disease. He could not avert his eyes from the modern town, as Wordsworth did, because the modern town meant a

great deal to him, and all of it was
intolerable. He observed that the dis-
appearance of beauty in human produc-
tions synchronised with the invention of
machinery and the development of great
industries, and he could not doubt that
the two changes were interconnected.
We sometimes forget that until the reign
of George III a town was regarded as
improving a landscape. A city was a
glorious and beautiful thing, an object to
be proud of. The hill of Zion is a fair
place, the joy of the whole earth, because
it had the holy city built upon it. Never
since civilisation began has such ugliness
been created as the modern English or
American town. Ruskin saw in these
structures a true index of the mind of
their builders and inhabitants, and the
sight filled him with horror. He read
with entire approval what Plato wrote
of industrialised Athens. 'The city of
which we are speaking,' he says in the
*Laws*, 'is some eighty furlongs from
the sea. Then there is some hope that
your citizens may be virtuous. Had you
been on the sea, and well provided with

harbours, and an importing rather than a producing country, some mighty saviour would have been needed, and lawgivers more than mortal, if you were to have even a chance of preserving your State from degeneracy. The sea is pleasant enough as a daily companion, but it has a bitter and brackish quality, filling the streets with merchants and shopkeepers, and begetting in the souls of men uncertain and dishonest ways, making the State unfaithful and unfriendly to her own children and to other nations.' Like Plato, Ruskin would fain have returned to a much simpler social structure, when each country, and even to a great extent each village, was sufficient to itself. He did not show how such a return is possible without blowing up the great towns and their inhabitants; but he quite seriously regarded the Industrial Revolution as a gigantic blunder, and believed that England would never be healthy or happy until what his contemporaries called progress had been somehow swept away with all its works. How this was to be done he hardly considered. Like a true Platonist, he set before his countrymen, in glowing language, the beauty of the eternal Ideas or absolute Values, pleaded that there was no necessary connection between equality of production and equality of remuneration, and instituted various experiments, not all unsuccessful, in restoring the old handicrafts and the temper which inspired them.

The problem of mending or ending industrialism, foolishly called capitalism, remains unsolved. Ruskin's own artistic life would have been impossible without the paternal sherry and the rich men who drank it; and Morris' exquisite manufactures depended absolutely on the patronage of the capitalists whom he denounced. But the indignation which these Victorian social reformers exhibited had much justification, even after the worst abuses had been partially remedied.

A mixture of rapid progress and extreme departmental inefficiency is one of the characteristics of the earlier part of the reign. Lord Justice Bowen has written an instructive sketch of the administration of the Law between 1837 and 1887. There were two systems of judicature, Law and Equity, with a different origin, different procedure, and different rules of right and wrong. One side of Westminster Hall gave judgments which the other side restrained the successful party from enforcing. The bewildered litigant was driven backwards and forwards. Merchants were hindered for months and years from recovering their dues. The fictitious adventures of John Doe and Richard Roe, the legal Gog and Magog, played an important part in trials to recover possession of land. Arrears accumulated year by year. The Court of Chancery was closed to the poor, and was a name of terror to the rich. It was said by a legal writer that 'no man can enter into a Chancery suit with any reasonable hope of being alive at its termination, if he has a determined adversary.' Bowen says that Dickens' pictures of the English law 'contain genuine history.' The horrors of the debtors' prison are well known, and nearly 4000 persons were sometimes arrested for debt in one year. In 1836,

494 persons were condemned to death, though only 34 were hanged. Public executions continued to 1867. If a farmer's gig knocked down a foot passenger in a lonely lane, two persons were not allowed to speak in court—the farmer and the pedestrian. Most of these abuses were rectified long before the end of the reign.

The Universities were slowly emerging from the depths to which they had sunk in the eighteenth century, when they neither taught nor examined nor maintained discipline. We all remember Gibbon's description of the Fellows of his College, 'whose dull but deep potations excused the brisker intemperance of youth.' These gentlemen were most of them waiting for College livings, to which they were allowed to carry off, as a solatium, some dozens of College port. Cambridge, it is only fair to say, never fell quite so low as Oxford, and began to reform itself earlier. The Mathematical and Classical Triposes were both founded before Queen Victoria's accession. But public opinion thought that the Uni-

versity authorities needed some stimula-
tion from outside, and in 1850 a Royal
Commission was appointed for Oxford,
and two years later another for Cambridge.
The Reports of these two Commissions
are very amusing, especially that of the
Oxford Board, which lets itself go in a
refreshing style. Its members had received
provocation. The Governing Bodies generally refused to answer their questions.
Some of the Colleges had exacted an oath
from new Fellows to reveal nothing about
the affairs of the College. The Dean of
Christ Church declined to answer letters
from the Royal Commission; the Presi-
dent of Magdalen replied that he was not
aware that he had misused his revenues,
and begged to close the correspondence.
These dignified potentates are not spared
in the Report. The Cambridge Report,
which is much more polite, did good
service by recommending the foundation
of a medical school. Changes later, such
as the abolition of all Anglican privileges,
and the permission of Fellows to marry,
came later. In the case of the Universities,
as in that of the Law, the improvements

between 1837 and the first Jubilee were enormous.

The Civil Service, it is almost needless to say, was a sanctuary of aristocratic jobbery. The Clerks were languid gentlemen with long whiskers, who arrived late and departed early from their Offices.

The Army in 1837 consisted, in actual strength, of about 100,000 men, of whom 19,000 were in India and 20,000 in Ireland. There had been a strong movement after the peace to abolish the army altogether, on the ground that another war was almost unthinkable. The Duke of Wellington was only able to keep up this small force by hiding it away in distant parts of the empire; the total number of troops in Great Britain was only 26,000. Officers were ordered to efface themselves by never wearing uniform except on parade. A Royal Duke could not be given a military funeral, because 'there were not troops enough to bury a Field Marshal.' As to the quality of the troops, the Duke frequently called them 'the scum of the earth,' and the brutal discipline of the time did everything to justify this description, for the soldier was supposed to have surrendered all his rights as a man and a citizen. The privates enlisted for life or for twenty-one years, and it was so difficult to get recruits that they were frequently caught while drunk, or frankly kidnapped. They were dressed, for campaigning in the tropics, in high leather stocks and buttoned up jackets, so that hundreds died of heat apoplexy. Lord Wolseley thinks that in 1837 50,000 Frenchmen could have easily taken London. Nor was the danger of a French invasion at all remote. The Volunteer movement, the social effects of which were excellent, was mainly due to the Prince Consort, a far wiser man than was recognised during his lifetime.

The Crimean War revealed in glaring colours the incompetence of the military authorities and of the Cabinet at home. If we had been fighting against any European power except Russia, with whom utter mismanagement is a tradition, there can be no doubt that our army would have been destroyed, as it ought to have been at Inkerman. The military credit of the nation was only partially restored by the prompt suppression of the Indian Mutiny. Yet here again the age of hope and progress made good its professions. The mistakes in the Boer War seem not to have been nearly so bad as those in the Crimea.

It would be easy to go through the other departments of national life—the Navy, Finance, Colonial and Indian Policy, the growth and distribution of Wealth, Locomotion and Transport, Education, Science, Medicine and Surgery, and to prove that the progress during the reign of Queen Victoria was quite unprecedented. The creed of optimism was natural and inevitable at such a time, though cool heads might remember the line of Publilius Syrus,

> Ubi nil timetur, quod timeatur nascitur.

Lecky, a historian with some practical experience of politics, deliberately stated his opinion that no country was ever better governed than England between 1832 and 1867, the dates of the first

Reform Bill and of Disraeli's scheme to
dish the Whigs. As far as internal affairs
go, it would not be easy to prove him
wrong. The one prime necessity for
good government was present ; those
who paid the taxes were also those who
imposed them. If there was some false
economy, as there was in the Crimean
War, sound finance benefited the whole
population by keeping credit high,
interest low, and taxation light. Political
life was purer than it had been, and
purer probably than it is now. The
House of Commons enjoyed that im-
mense prestige which has been com-
pletely lost since the old Queen's death.
The debates were read with semi-religious
fervour by every good citizen over his
breakfast, and a prominent politician was
treated with even more exaggerated
reverence than our worthy grandfathers
paid to bishops. The debates were good
because they were real debates and con-
ducted by men who all spoke the same
language. The rhetorical methods of the
working man are quite different from
those of the gentry, and mutual annoyance

is generated by the mixture of styles
in debate. Above all, the House of
Commons was still a rather independent
body. The history of England shows that
as soon as the Commons freed themselves from the control of the king, they
began to try to free themselves from
the control of the constituencies. They
debated in secret; they made their persons legally sacrosanct; and on several
occasions they turned out a member who
had been duly elected by his constituents,
and admitted a member who had been
duly rejected. These encroachments
could not last long. The Bradlaugh case
was the last attempt to repeat the tactics
by which Wilkes was kept out of Parliament; but until the poisonous delegate
theory obtained currency, the member
of Parliament was a real legislator, with
a right to think, speak and vote for himself. During the middle part of the reign,
the dramatic duel between Gladstone
and Disraeli gave a heroic aspect to party
politics, and kept up the public interest.

In foreign politics it is not so easy to
share Lecky's opinion. The opium war

against China, and the Crimean War, were blunders which hardly anyone now defends; and Palmerston's habit of bullying weak foreign powers did not really raise our prestige. For a long time we could not make up our minds whether France or Russia was the potential enemy; a vacillation which proved that the balance of power, which we thought so necessary for our safety, already existed. Our statesmen were blind to the menace from Germany, down to the end of the reign and later. The Crimean War only increased the friction between France and England. The French fortified Cherbourg, and talked openly of invasion. In 1860 Flahault, the French ambassador in London, said bluntly that 'his great object was to prevent war between the two countries.'

This prolonged jealousy and suspicion between the two western powers made it impossible for England to exercise much influence on the Continent. The settlement after 1815 handed over central and eastern Europe to governments of the type which it is the fashion to call reactionary. Russia, Prussia, and Austria, acting together, were not to be resisted. And so the disturbances of 1848, once more kindled by Paris, just failed; and democracy had a serious rebuff. Nearly all the despotic governments of Europe were overthrown in 1848, and nearly all were restored a year later. The French indeed got rid of their king, mainly because he was a pacifist; but Germany refused to be unified under the red flag, and began to prepare for a very different destiny. The Pope wobbled and then came down heavily on the side of the old order. Meanwhile, England looked on. Chartism was a very feeble affair compared to the continental revolutions, and it flickered out in this year. The people had got rid of the corn-laws, and were fairly content; there was nothing at all like a class war in this generation. So, while Macaulay was showing how very differently we manage things in England—compare, for example, 1688 with 1848—we decided to invite the world and his wife to London, to envy and admire us in Sir Joseph Paxton's

great glass house. We must not laugh
at that architectural monstrosity. It was
the mausoleum of certain generous hopes.
On the Continent men had been shot
and hanged for the brotherhood of the
human race; we hoped to show them a
more excellent way. We had given a lead
in free trade; we still hoped that our
example would soon be followed in all
civilised nations. We had reduced our
army to almost nothing; we hoped that
militarism was a thing of the past. All
these hopes were frustrated. A fanatical
nationalism began to foster racial ani-
mosity; the *enragés* of Europe began to
preach class-hatred and to find many
listeners; protective tariffs were set up
on every frontier; international law became a mere cloak for the schemes of
violence; and, as has been said, all Europe
'breathed a harsher air.' Worst of all,
the mad race of competitive armaments,
which was destined to wreck a great part
of the wealth which two generations of
peaceful industry had gathered, was begun.

We have to remember that the prosperity and security of the happy time

which we are now considering were due
to temporary causes, which can never
recur. In the nineteenth century England
was the most fortunately situated country,
geographically, in the world. When the
opening and development of the Atlantic
trade deprived the Mediterranean ports
of their pride of place, an Atlantic stage
of world-commerce began, in which
England, an island with good harbours
on its western coasts, was in the most
favourable position. The Pacific stage
which is now beginning must inevitably
give the primacy to America. We had
also a long start, industrially, over all
our rivals, and our possession of great
coal-fields and iron-fields close together
gave us a still further advantage. Our
labour was then cheap and good ; our
manufacturers capable and energetic.
All these advantages are past or passing.
Henceforth we shall have to compete
with other nations on unprivileged conditions. It is useless to lament the inevitable, but it is foolish to shut our
eyes to it. The Victorian Age was the
culminating point of our prosperity.

Our great wealth, indeed, continued to advance till the catastrophe of 1914. But there was a shadow of apprehension over everything—'never glad confident morning again.'

Let us now turn to the intellectual and spiritual movements of the reign. The Romanticist revolution was complete, in a sense, before 1825. It was a European, not only an English movement, and perhaps it was not less potent in France than in Germany and England, though in accordance with the genius and traditions of that nation it took very different forms. In England it inspired verse more than prose, though we must not forget Scott's novels. It produced a galaxy of great poetry during the Great War, and added another immortal glory to that age of heroic struggle. By a strange chance, nearly all the great poets of the war-period died young. Wordsworth alone was left, and he was spared to reap in a barren old age the honours which he had earned and not received between 1798 and 1820. For about fifteen years there was an interregnum in English literature, which makes a convenient division between the great men of the Napoleonic era and the great Victorians.

From about 1840, when great literature again began to appear, the conditions were more like those with which we are familiar. There was an unparalleled output of books of all kinds, a very large reading public, and a steadily increasing number of professional authors dependent on the success of their popular appeal. As in our own day, a great quantity of good second-rate talent trod on the heels of genius, and made it more difficult for really first-rate work to find recognition. The impetus of the Romantic movement was by no means exhausted, but it began to spread into new fields. The study of 'Gothic' art and literature had been at first, as was inevitable, ill-informed. Its reconstruction of the Middle Ages was a matter of sentimental antiquarianism, no more successful than much of its church restoration. The Victorians now extended the imaginative sensibility which had been expended on nature and history, to the life of the individual. This meant that the novel instead of the poem was to be the characteristic means of literary expression ; and even the chief Victorian poets, Tennyson and Browning, are sometimes novelists in verse.

The grandest and most fully representative figure in all Victorian literature is of course Alfred Tennyson. And here let me digress for one minute. It was a good rule of Thomas Carlyle to set a portrait of the man whom he was describing in front of him on his writing-table. It is a practice which would greatly diminish the output of literary impertinence. Let those who are disposed to follow the present evil fashion of disparaging the great Victorians make a collection of their heads in photographs or engravings, and compare them with those of their own little favourites. Let them set up in a row good portraits of Tennyson, Charles Darwin, Gladstone, Manning, Newman, Martineau, Lord Lawrence, Burne Jones, and, if they like, a dozen lesser luminaries, and ask

themselves candidly whether men of this
stature are any longer among us. I will
not speculate on the causes which from
time to time throw up a large number
of great men in a single generation. I
will only ask you to agree with me that
since the golden age of Greece (assuming
that we can trust the portrait busts of
the famous Greeks) no age can boast so
many magnificent types of the human
countenance as the reign of Queen Victoria. We, perhaps, being epigoni ourselves, are more at home among our
fellow-pygmies. Let us agree with Ovid,
if we will:

Prisca iuvent alios; ego me nunc denique natum
    Gratulor; haec aetas moribus apta meis.

But let us have the decency to uncover
before the great men of the last century;
and if we cannot appreciate them, let
us reflect that the fault may possibly be
in ourselves.

Tennyson's leonine head realises the
ideal of a great poet. And he reigned
nearly as long as his royal mistress. The
longevity and unimpaired freshness of

the great Victorians has no parallel in history, except in ancient Greece. The great Attic tragedians lived as long as Tennyson and Browning; the Greek philosophers reached as great ages as Victorian theologians; but if you look at the dates in other flowering times of literature you will find that the life of a man of genius is usually short, and his period of production very short indeed.

Tennyson is now depreciated for several reasons. His technique as a writer of verse was quite perfect; our newest poets prefer to write verses which will not even scan. He wrote beautifully about beautiful things, and among beautiful things he included beautiful conduct. He thought it an ugly and disgraceful thing for a wife to be unfaithful to her husband, and condemned Guinevere and Lancelot as any sound moralist would condemn them. A generation which will not buy a novel unless it contains some scabrous story of adultery, and revels in the 'realism' of the man with a muck-rake, naturally 'has no use for' the *Idylls of the King*, and calls Arthur the blameless prig. The reaction against Tennyson has culminated in abuse of the Idylls, in which the present generation finds all that it most dislikes in the Victorian mind. Modern research has unburied the unsavoury story that Modred was the illegitimate son of Arthur by his own half-sister, and blames Tennyson for not treating the whole story as an Oedipus-legend. In reality, Malory does not so treat it. He admits the story, but depicts Arthur as the flower of kinghood, 'Rex quondam rexque futurus.' Tennyson, however, was not bound to follow Malory. He has followed other and still greater models, Spenser and Milton. He has given us an allegorical epic, as he explains in his Epilogue to the Queen:

> Accept this old imperfect tale,
> New-old, and shadowing Sense at war with Soul,
> Ideal manhood closed in real man
> Rather than that gray king, whose name, a ghost,
> Streams like a cloud, man-shaped, from mountain peak,
> And cleaves to cairn and cromlech still; or him
> Of Geoffrey's book, or him of Malleor's.

The whole poem is an allegory. Camelot is

> Never built at all,
> And therefore built for ever.

The charming novelettes in which the allegory is forgotten need no more justification than the adventures in *The Faerie Queene*, or the parliamentary debates in *Paradise Lost*. The Idylls fall into line with two of the greatest poems in the English language; and when Tennyson writes of Arthur, 'From the great deep to the great deep he goes,' he is telling his own deepest conviction of what our brief life on earth means—the conviction which inspires his last words of poetry, *Crossing the Bar*.

Tennyson knew materialism and revolution, and whither they tend.

> The children born of thee are sword and fire,
> Red ruin, and the breaking up of laws.

And

> The fear lest this my realm, upreared
> By noble needs at one with noble vows,
> From flat confusion and brute violence
> Reel back into the beast and be no more.

We are told that he is shallow, an echo of the thoughts of educated men at the time, and that, like the Victorians in general, he never probes anything to the bottom. It is true that he reflects his age; so do almost all other great men; and that his age was an age of transition; so, I believe, are all other ages. He represents his age both in his deep-rooted conservatism or moderate liberalism, and in his reverence for the new knowledge which was undermining the conservative stronghold, especially in religion. He is unjustly reproached with speaking contemptuously of the French Revolution, 'the red fool-fury of the Celt,' as 'no graver than a schoolboys' barring out.' He despised barricades and red flags and September massacres, because he believed that the victories of broadening Freedom are to be won by constitutional means. He is a little self-righteous about it, no doubt; that helps to date him. He came, we must remember, half-way between the Pantisocracy of Coleridge and his friends and the still cruder vagaries of our young intellectuals. Years brought the philosophic mind to Carlyle, Southey, Wordsworth and Coleridge. Years will bring a relative sanity to our young Bolsheviks; they will then, I hope (for I wish them well), begin to read Tennyson.

The second *Locksley Hall* is peculiarly interesting for our purpose, because, though the author protested that it was written in character, dramatically, it is plain that it does express his political and social disillusionments and anxiety about the future; and Gladstone answered it as an attack upon the England of the day, calling attention to the great progress which had been made in the 'sixty years' since the first *Locksley Hall.* Tennyson saw that the Victorian social order was breaking up; and with great prescience he foretold many of the evils which have since come upon us. The deluge of political 'babble'; the ghastly cruelties of the Irish; the indifference of the new voters to the British Empire; the contempt for experience and wisdom, setting the feet above the brain and bringing back the dark ages without their faith or hope; the vague aspirations for international friendship, blighted by the pressure of over-population and ending in universal war; all these shadows of coming events, too clearly seen, have convinced him that there is no straight line of progress, but many a backward-streaming curve, which often seems more like retrogression than progress. This is not the language of 1851. In truth the clouds began to gather before the old Queen and the old poet died. Even in fiction, the note of disillusionment is heard with increasing clearness, in the latest novels of George Eliot, in writers like Gissing, and in the later books of Thomas Hardy compared with the earlier.

In religion Tennyson certainly represents the mood of the mid-century. Romanticism had given religion a new attractiveness in the revolutionary era. In France it stimulated the Neo-Catholicism of De Maistre and Chateaubriand; in Germany it gave a mystical turn to philosophical idealism; and in England it produced an Anglo-Catholic revival. But for reasons mentioned above, this revival remained intensely insular. England, and perhaps especially Oxford, were at this time so cut off from the Continent that the isolation of the English Tractarians was not at first felt;

and the constructive work of philosophers and critics on the Continent was spurned as 'German theology.' So when Newman at length took the perhaps logical step of joining the Roman communion, the movement broke up, and its ablest members turned against it with the anger of men who feel that they have been duped. Neither science nor criticism could be disregarded any longer. English scholars began to read German, as Carlyle had exhorted them to do; and everybody began to read Darwin. There arose among the educated class an attitude towards religion which we may call very distinctively Victorian. Carlyle remained a Puritan, without any dogmatic beliefs except a kind of moralistic pantheism. Ruskin was a Protestant medievalist, who admired everything in a medieval cathedral except the altar. Tennyson and Browning were ready to let most dogmas go, but clung passionately to the belief in personal human survival. Tennyson's famous lines 'There lives more faith in honest doubt, Believe me, than in half the creeds' have been

wittily parodied by Samuel Butler:
'There lives more doubt in honest faith'
etc. The sentiment in Tennyson's lines
may be easily defended; but it must be
confessed that 'honest doubt' was something of a pose at the time. In reading
such men as Clough, or Henri Amiel,
the average man becomes impatient, and
is inclined to say 'Why can't the fellow
make up his mind one way or the other,
and get started?' They carry suspension
of judgment to the verge of futility, and
though they obviously suffer, one does
not feel very sorry for them. It is the
opposite failing from that of Macaulay,
who as a historian suffers from a constitutional inability *not* to make up his mind
on everything and everybody. Matthew
Arnold is also a religious sceptic; but
he has formulated a liberal Protestant
creed for himself, not very unlike that of
Sir John Seeley's 'Ecce Homo.' It was
not a happy time for religious thinkers,
unless they made themselves quite independent of organised Christianity.
Intolerance was very bitter; and only the
secular arm stopped a whole series of

ecclesiastical prosecutions, which would have made the ministry of the Church of England impossible except for fools, liars, and bigots. Real hatred was shown against the scientific leaders, which Darwin calmly ignored, and Huxley returned with interest.

But though the contradictions and perplexities of rapid transition were more felt in religion than in any other subject, it may be doubted whether organised Christianity has ever been more influential in England than during the Victorian age, before the growth of the towns threw all the Church's machinery out of gear. Many of you will remember Lecky's charming description of the typical country parsonage, and the gracious and civilising influences which radiated from what was often the very ideal of a Christian home. The description is in no way exaggerated; and now that high prices and predatory taxation have destroyed this pleasant and unique feature of English life, it is worth while to recall to the younger generation what it was in the time of their fathers and grandfathers.

I have taken Tennyson as my example of Victorian literature, because his is the greatest and most representative name. It is no reproach to say that he is thoroughly English. Browning is more cosmopolitan, but his method of facing the problems of life like a bull at a fence is characteristically English.

There is no time to speak at length of the Victorian novel, another bright star in the firmament of the reign. Our nation has a great tradition in fiction, and we shall be wise to stick to it, instead of preferring a corrupt following of the French, whose novelists, in spite of their clever technique, seem to me frequently dull and usually repulsive. Dickens and Thackeray have been rivals, almost like Gladstone and Disraeli, and perhaps few are whole-hearted admirers of both. That any educated reader should fail to love one or the other is to me inexplicable. The palmiest day of English novel-writing was in the fifties, when Dickens, Thackeray, Charlotte Brontë, George Eliot, Anthony Trollope, Kingsley, Disraeli, Bulwer Lytton and Meredith were all writing. Later in the reign there was a short set-back, and the fortunes of English fiction seemed for a few years to be less promising than they became in the next generation, when several new writers of great ability and charm appeared. Now we seem to be once more in the trough of the wave; and I cannot doubt that the main cause of the decay is the pernicious habit of writing hastily for money. If we take the trouble to consult Mr Mudie's catalogue of fiction, we shall learn to our amazement that there are several writers, whose names we have never heard, who have to their discredit over a hundred works of fiction apiece. They obviously turn out several books a year, just as a shoemaker manufactures so many pairs of boots. The great novelists have generally written rapidly, rather too rapidly; but such a cataract of ink as these heroes of the circulating library spill is absolutely inconsistent with even second-rate work. Literature flourishes best when it is half a trade and half an art; and here again the Victorian Age occupies the most favourable part of the curve.

Of the other glories of Victorian literature I can say nothing now. But before leaving this part of the subject, consider the wonderful variety of strong or beautiful English prose writing which that age produced. Froude, Macaulay, Newman, Ruskin, Pater and Stevenson are each supreme in very different styles; and all of them achieved excellence by an amount of labour which very few writers are now willing to bestow.

I have no wish to offer an unmeasured panegyric on an age which after all cannot be divested of the responsibility for making our own inevitable. It was to a considerable extent vulgarised by the amazing success of the Industrial Revolution. Napoleon's nation of shopkeepers did judge almost everything by quantitative standards, and by quantitative standards the higher values cannot be measured. There was no lack of prophets to point out a better way, but the nation as a whole was not unfairly caricatured as John Bull, that stout, comfortable, rather bullying figure which excited Ruskin's indignation, and which others

have said that we ought to burn instead
of Guy Fawkes. We were unpopular
on the Continent just when we thought
that all other nations were envying us.
They did envy us; but with the under-
lying conviction that there must be
something wrong in a world where the
Palmerstonian John Bull comes out top.

The greatness of the age, as I have
said, depended on a combination of cir-
cumstances in their nature transient. It
resembled the short-lived greatness of
Venice, Genoa, and Holland. Before the
end of the reign society had begun to
disintegrate, so that we find antagonistic
movements flourishing together. Theo-
retical socialism reached its zenith; but
there was also an outburst of romantic
imperialism, of which Sir John Seeley,
Regius Professor of History at Cambridge,
was one of the founders, Froude and Dilke
powerful propagandists, Rudyard Kipling
the poet, and Joseph Chamberlain the
practical manager. It was a mild attack
of the epidemic which afterwards enticed
Germany into the Great War, and the
worst that can be said of it is that it en-

couraged a temper of sentimental brutalism in the English people, and brought us for the first time into danger from a coalition of foreign powers. The second Jubilee was its day of triumph ; the Boer War the beginning of its downfall.

The fusion of social classes proceeded more and more rapidly as the century went on. At the beginning of the reign the territorial oligarchs purchased another lease of power by an alliance with the successful commercial class which, with the Indian Nabobs, had been violently radical until the aristocracy recognised them. The two parties quarrelled about the Corn Laws and Factory Acts, but when these questions were settled, they gradually drew together, while lavish new creations of peers turned the House of Lords into the predominantly middle class body which it is now. Towards the end of the reign the higher gentry began again to go into trade, as they had done until the Georges brought in German ideas, and the way was prepared for the complete destruction of social barriers which the Great War effected. Meanwhile,

there were ominous signs that our civilisation, like others in the past, might be
poisoned by the noxious by-products of
its own activities. Parasitism at both ends
of the scale, but far most at the lower,
became an ever-increasing burden on industry, and symptoms of race-deteriora-
tion became apparent to the very few who
have eyes for such things. Legislation
removed most of the obvious evils in the
workmen's lot, but one evil it could not
remove, and this became more grievous
and more resented every year. The great
industry was turning human beings into
mere cogs in machines, and as mechanism
every year tended to supplant manual
skill, the clever craftsman of the past was
functionally obsolescent, and a type of
workman was evolved who needed no
craftsmanship such as an intelligent man
could be proud to acquire and happy to
exercise. This problem, which threatens
the life of our civilisation, was already
beginning to loom darkly before the eyes
of the late Victorians.

I have no doubt that the Elizabethan
and the Victorian Ages will appear to the

historian of the future as the twin peaks in which English civilisation culminated. The twentieth century will doubtless be full of interest, and may even develop some elements of greatness. But as regards the fortunes of this country, the signs are that our work on a grand scale, with the whole world as our stage, is probably nearing its end. Europe has sacrificed its last fifty years of primacy by an insane and suicidal struggle. America has emerged as the *tertius gaudens*. Where shall we be thirty years hence? It is for you, my younger hearers, to answer that question, for the answer depends on yourselves. We old Victorians will before then have made room for you by quitting a world to which, as I am sure you think, we no longer belong.

Lightning Source UK Ltd.
Milton Keynes UK
UKHW010628031120
372707UK00001B/72

9 781107 495098